IELTS Listening Practice Tests:

IELTS Exam Preparation Book with 4 Practice Tests, Free mp3s and Tips for a High Score

NOTE: IELTS is jointly owned by the British Council, IDP: IELTS Australia, and Cambridge English Language Assessments, which are neither affiliated with nor endorse this publication.

IELTS Listening Practice Tests: IELTS Exam Preparation Book with 4 Practice Tests, Free mp3s and Tips for a High Score

© COPYRIGHT 1995, 2014, 2021. IELTS Success Associates dba www.examsam.com

All rights reserved. No part of this publication may be reproduced, stored in a retrieval system, or transmitted, in any form or by any means, electronic, mechanical, photocopying, recording or otherwise.

ISBN: 978-1-949282-79-5

COPYRIGHT NOTICE TO EDUCATORS: Please respect copyright law. Under no circumstances may you make copies of these materials for distribution to or use by students. Should you wish to use the materials with students, you are required to purchase a copy of this publication for each of your students.

NOTE: IELTS is jointly owned by the British Council, IDP: IELTS Australia, and Cambridge English Language Assessments, which are neither affiliated with nor endorse this publication.

TABLE OF CONTENTS

IELTS Listening Exam Information   1

Instructions to Candidates – IELTS Listening   2

IELTS Listening Exam Format   3

IELTS Listening Exam Question Types   4

How to Use This Publication   5

Instructions on How to Access the Free mp3s   5

IELTS Practice Listening – Test 1 Answer Sheet   6

IELTS Practice Listening – Test 1:

    Section 1   7

    Section 2   10

    Section 3   13

    Section 4   15

Answer Key – Listening Practice Test 1   17

Texts, Answers and Explanations – Practice Listening Test 1:

    Section 1   20

    Section 2   26

    Section 3   32

    Section 4   36

IELTS Practice Listening – Test 2 Answer Sheet   41

IELTS Practice Listening – Test 2:

    Section 1   42

    Section 2   44

    Section 3   46

    Section 4   49

Answer Key – Listening Practice Test 2   50

Texts, Answers and Explanations – Practice Listening Test 2:

    Section 1   52

    Section 2   57

    Section 3   63

    Section 4   70

IELTS Practice Listening – Test 3 Answer Sheet   75

IELTS Practice Listening – Test 3:

    Section 1   76

    Section 2   78

    Section 3   80

    Section 4   83

Answer Key – Listening Practice Test 3   86

Texts, Answers and Explanations – Practice Listening Test 3:

    Section 1   88

    Section 2   93

    Section 3   100

    Section 4   106

IELTS Practice Listening – Test 1 Answer Sheet   112

IELTS Practice Listening – Test 4:

    Section 1   113

    Section 2   115

    Section 3   118

    Section 4   120

Answer Key – Listening Practice Test 4   122

Texts, Answers and Explanations – Practice Listening Test 4:

    Section 1   124

    Section 2   128

    Section 3   132

    Section 4   136

IELTS Listening Exam Information

The listening part of the IELTS test is the same for the General Training Module as it is for the Academic Module.

You can therefore use this publication to prepare for either the IELTS for Academic Purposes Exam or the IELTS General Training Exam.

The IELTS listening test normally lasts for about 30 minutes.

When the test finishes, you will be given 10 more minutes in order to write your answers on the answer sheet provided.

The IELTS listening test has four parts. There are 40 questions in total on the listening test and each question is worth one point.

For each section of the listening test, you will be given time to look through the questions before listening to the recording. You will also have time to check your answers when the recording finishes.

You will hear the recordings ONLY ONCE.

As you complete the practice listening tests in this book, you should go quickly from one section to the next in order to make your testing practice as realistic as possible.

Read the instructions for each section of the test and be sure that you answer all of the questions.

When you have completed each practice listening test, check your answers and study the explanations provided.

Instructions to Candidates – IELTS Listening

On the real IELTS test, you will see instructions like the following:

- Do not open the test booklet until you are instructed to begin the exam.

- Write your candidate number and name at the top of your answer sheet.

- Listen to the instructions carefully.

- Be sure to answer all the questions.

- While listening, you should write your answers on the exam booklet.

- You will be given 10 minutes to copy your answers onto the answer sheet when the recordings have finished.

- Use a pencil to write your answers on the answer sheet.

- You will then be asked to hand in your question paper and answer sheet.

- Your score will be based only on the answer sheet.

- The examiners do not consider notes or answers that you may have written on the test itself.

IELTS Listening Exam Format

There are five formats of questions on the IELTS listening test:

1) Multiple choice questions – you will need to choose the correct answer from options A, B or C.

2) Form or diagram completion – you will see a form or diagram and will have to fill in the missing information.

3) Matching – you will need to choose 2 or more answers from the choices provided.

4) Short answers – you will see a question and an empty line on which to write your answer. No word limit will be given for your response.

5) Sentence completion – you will see a gap in a sentence and instructions telling you how many words to place in the gap. For these questions, it is very important not to exceed the limit. If you place more words in the gap than permitted, you will receive a score of zero for that question.

IELTS Listening Exam Question Types

Listening questions on the IELTS test can be placed into three broad categories:

1) Main idea questions – For these types of questions, you will need to understand the main idea or "gist" of the conversation or lecture.

2) Specific detail questions – The majority of questions on the listening test are this type. You will need to identify a specific point from the recording.

3) Intonation – These questions will ask you to infer the speaker's attitude from his or her tone or emphasis.

How to Use This Publication

The listening practice tests in this publication contain questions of all of the formats and types that you will see on the real test.

As you complete the practice tests in this book, you should pay special attention to the tips at the beginning of each section of practice test 1. Although you will not see tips like this on the actual exam, these tips will help you improve your performance on each subsequent practice test in this publication.

You should also study the explanations to the answers to listening practice test 1 especially carefully.

The tips that you will see in the questions and the explanations to the first practice test will help you obtain strategies to improve your performance on the other listening practice tests in this book.

Of course, these strategies will also help you do your best on the day of your actual test.

Instructions on How to Access the Free mp3s:

To open the free sound files that accompany these practice tests, please go to: **https://item1093.examsam.com**

IELTS Practice Listening – Test 1
Answer Sheet

1.	21.
2.	22.
3.	23.
4.	24.
5.	25.
6.	26.
7.	27.
8.	28.
9.	29.
10.	30.
11.	31.
12.	32.
13.	33.
14.	34.
15.	35.
16.	36.
17.	37.
18.	38.
19.	39.
20.	40.

IELTS Practice Listening – Test 1

LISTENING PRACTICE TEST 1

> **Tip:** Questions 1 to 10 are multiple choice questions. Remember to select an answer, even if you are not confident about your choice. Even if you are not sure about the answer, you will have a 33.33% chance of being correct.

SECTION 1   **QUESTIONS 1 – 10**

Choose the correct letter A, B or C

1) How long ago was the student absent?
   - A. a couple of weeks
   - B. three weeks
   - C. a couple of months

2) The professor is surprised because
   - A. the student asked to speak to him.
   - B. the student delayed speaking to him.
   - C. the student asked him to repeat the attendance policy.

Continued on next page.

3) Why did the student miss class?
   A. She misunderstood the policy on attendance.
   B. She didn't know what time the class met.
   C. She has a medical problem.

4) The student is worried because
   A. she thinks she missed information that will be on the test.
   B. she knows the exam is comprehensive.
   C. she realised she has embarrassed the professor.

5) Based upon the professor's tone of voice at the beginning of the discussion, what can be understood about his attitude?
   A. He is upset about the policy that the university has established.
   B. He realised that the attendance policy is confusing for students.
   C. He feels a little bit annoyed with the student.

6) What does the professor mean when he says the following?: "We will have to give you more leeway".
   A. The professor will be more flexible with the student.
   B. The professor is saying that there is no excuse for the absence.
   C. The professor is saying that the university will consider the case carefully.

7) What solution did the professor suggest to the student?
   A. To complete an additional assignment in lieu of the lecture.
   B. To arrange for another student to share his or her notes.
   C. To provide the student with copies of the PowerPoint slides.

Continued on next page.

8) What information is on the final exam?
    A. anything covered in the class
    B. anything covered in the homework
    C. only the information that the professor specifies

9) What homework did the student miss?
    A. an exam
    B. a note-taking exercise
    C. a 300-word assignment

10) What does the professor ask for as evidence?
    A. a personal response letter
    B. a doctor's note
    C. a medical examination

SECTION 2   QUESTIONS 11 – 20

> **Tips:** Questions 11 to 16 are form-completion questions. Most of the questions on form completion will ask for specific details. Remember to write what you hear, even if you are not sure about the spelling. The instructions for the questions in this section tell you to put ONE word in each gap, so do not write more than one word for these questions.

Questions 11-16

*Complete the form below. Write **ONLY ONE WORD** in each gap.*

Student Accommodation Request Form	
Current Residence	**11)** _____ Hall
What does the student request? *(Put one word in each gap)*	**12)** _____ to a **13)** _____ residential hall
Is the student's request a "compelling case"? *(Tick one box)*	**14)** ☐ ☐ YES NO
Reason for the request *(Put one word in each gap)*	Too **15)** _____ in the room. Difficult to **16)** _____ .

Tip: Questions 17 and 18 are short-answer questions. The instructions for questions 17 and 18 tell you to put no more than two words in each gap, so do not put in more than two words for the responses to each of these two questions.

Questions 17-18

Answer the questions below. Write **NO MORE THAN TWO WORDS** *for each answer.*

17) Where does the accommodation officer recommend that the student study?

   _____

18) What is the name of the resident director?

   _____

Tip: Questions 19 and 20 are sentence-completion questions. Sentence completion questions are very similar to short-answer questions. Remember to keep your response within the word limit. Also remember that your response must be grammatically correct within the context of the sentence.

Questions 19-20

*Complete the sentences below. Write **NO MORE THAN TWO WORDS** for each answer.*

19) The student had not met the resident director because the student _____ .

20) If the other students ignore the resident director's warning, a(n) _____ can be filed against them.

SECTION 3   QUESTIONS 21 – 30

Tip: Questions 21 to 28 are form-completion questions. Remember that most of the questions on form completion tasks will ask for specific details from the recording. The missing specific details will often be names or dates, as is the case in this section of the practice test.

Questions 21-28

*Complete the notes below. Write **ONLY ONE WORD OR NUMBER** in each gap.*

TOPIC: The function of the human **21)** _____

Part I – Important Scientists:

Date: 1929 Name: Hans **22)** _____

His research was **23)** _____ by other scientists.

Date: **24)** _____   Name: Edgar Adrian

Nationality: **25)** _____

Discovered four **26)** _____ in the brain.

PART II – Measurement of Brain Activity:

CAT scan: Like an **27)** _____ of the brain.

28) _____ scan: Radioactive substance is used.

Tip: Questions 29 and 30 are classified as matching-type questions. You need to identify two items from the list as advantages of the CAT scan which were mentioned in the seminar.

Questions 29-30

What are two advantages of the CAT scan?

Choose two answers from the box and then write the letters next to questions 29 and 30.

> A. It is a cross-section.
>
> B. It is magnetic.
>
> C. It is less invasive than other scans.
>
> D. It is three dimensional.
>
> E. It appears in different colours.

29) _____

30) _____

SECTION 4   *QUESTIONS 31 – 40*

Tip: Questions 31 to 40 are form-completion questions. This form is in a table format. Look at the description in the left-hand column, and then complete the requested information in the right-hand column of the chart. Your word limit is only one word or number per gap for this part of the practice test.

Complete the chart below, using **NO MORE THAN TWO WORDS OR NUMBERS** for each gap.

\	HSBC Building Facts and Figures
Location	**31)** _____
Components and their country of origin	Windows: Austria Exterior walls: **32)** _____ Toilets & Air Conditioning: Japan Other components: **33)** _____ *Continued on next page.*

Advantage of prefabrication	Made the construction more **34)** _____
Number of storeys	**35)** _____
Special considerations	Disruption of ground **36)** _____ supply
Design	Number of columns: 8 Weight: more than **37)** _____ tonnes Further support provided by **38)** _____ beams Exteriors walls consist of: large panes of window **39)** _____ and **40)** _____ panels

ANSWER KEY – LISTENING PRACTICE TEST 1

1) B

2) B

3) B

4) A

5) C

6) A

7) C

8) A

9) C

10) B

11) Henderson

12) move

13) different

14) NO

15) noisy

16) read / write / study / concentrate

17) the library / library

18) John Marshall

19) arrived late / missed orientation

20) formal complaint

21) brain

22) Berger (Burger is also acceptable)

23) dismissed / disregarded

24) 1932

25) Briton / British

26) frequencies

27) X-ray / Xray

28) PET

29) A or C

30) C or A

31) Hong Kong

32) United States

33) Germany

34) efficient

35) 47

36) water

37) 1000

38) steel

39) glass

40) aluminium

TEXTS, ANSWERS AND EXPLANATIONS

LISTENING PRACTICE TEST 1

SECTION 1 – LISTENING TEXT

Student: Hi Professor Emerson. I know you're busy, but could I speak with you for a couple of seconds.

Teacher: No problem. Have a seat.

Student: The thing is, you know, I was absent three weeks ago, and I was wondering if I missed anything important.

Teacher: Yes, of course, all of the information conveyed in class is important! And to be honest, I'm quite surprised that you're asking about it only now.

Student: Sorry, I'm not following you.

Teacher: What I'm getting at is . . . I'm sure you remember at the beginning of each semester when I mentioned the policy on absences. I said then that a student needed to see me as soon as possible following an absence.

Student: Oh . . . yeah . . . I see what you mean. I just realised today, though, when you were talking about the test that's coming up next week

. . . I was worried about the session I missed, in case any of that information is on the exam.

Teacher: I can't reveal any information about what's going to be covered on the end-of-semester test. But I can tell you that it is a comprehensive test . . . Well . . . three weeks have passed since you missed the class . . . That's quite a long time, don't you think?

Student: Yeah . . . I'm a little bit embarrassed about it . . . That's why I hesitated to see you about the problem . . . Actually, I've just been diagnosed with diabetes. I've kind of been struggling the past couple of weeks to pay attention in class, because my medical condition makes me feel quite tired.

Teacher: Well . . . when a student has a medical condition, it is considered to be an extenuating circumstance, so we can excuse your absence. We will also have to give you more leeway . . . about your homework and so on.

Student: Oh . . . that's great news, because as I said, I've been finding it really difficult to concentrate.

Teacher: Well, as you know, I usually tell absent students to copy the lecture notes from a friend. But in your case, why don't I just give you a copy of my PowerPoint slides for the lecture that you missed. Would that be helpful?

Student: That would be great! Will any of the information from that lecture be on the test?

Teacher: As I said, I really can't give precise details about the final exam. But I would emphasize again, that it's a comprehensive test. So anything we have talked about in class can be included on the final exam.

Student: Okay, so I'll just review everything for the final test. Did I miss any homework?

Teacher: Actually, there was a 300-word personal response piece that's due next Tuesday. But if you can give me a note from your doctor as evidence of your medical condition, I can give you a two-week extension.

Student: No problem. I can bring the doctor's note to our next class. Is that okay?

Teacher: That would be fine. Here are copies of the PowerPoint slides . . . Is there anything else I can help you with?

Student: No, that's all. Thanks so much for your help.

Teacher: No problem at all. See you in class next week.

LISTENING PRACTICE TEST 1

SECTION 1 – ANSWERS AND EXPLANATIONS

1) The correct answer is B. This is a specific detail question. The student was absent three weeks ago. She says: "The thing is, you know, I was absent three weeks ago, and I was wondering if I missed anything important".

2) The correct answer is B. This is an intonation and emphasis question. The professor is surprised because the student delayed speaking to him. We know that the professor is surprised because he states: "To be honest, I'm quite surprised that you're asking about it only now". He later emphasizes the phrase "as soon as possible" by his intonation in order to imply that the student should not have delayed speaking to him. He does this when he tells the student: "I'm sure you remember at the beginning of each semester when I mentioned the policy on absences. I said then that a student needed to see me *as soon as possible* following an absence".

3) The correct answer is C. This is a specific detail question. The student missed class because she has a medical problem. She states: "Actually, I've just been diagnosed with diabetes. I've kind of been

struggling the past couple of weeks to pay attention in class, because my medical condition makes me feel quite tired".

4) The correct answer is A. This is another specific detail question. The student is worried because she thinks that she has missed information that will be on the test. We know that she is anxious because she asks: "Will any of the information from that lecture be on the test?"

5) The correct answer is C. This is another intonation and emphasis question. Based upon the professor's tone of voice at the beginning of the discussion, we can understand that he feels a little bit annoyed with the student. The professor implies that he is a bit irritated when he states: "Yes, of course, all of the information conveyed in class is important! And to be honest, I'm quite surprised that you're asking about it only now". His irritation is also evident a bit later when he tells the student: "Well . . . three weeks have passed since you missed the class . . . That's quite a long time, don't you think?"

6) The correct answer is A. This is a specific detail question that focuses on idiomatic usage. When the professor says: "We will have to give you more leeway", he means that he will be more flexible with the student. We can also understand this because the professor talks about "extenuating circumstances" in the previous sentence.

7) The correct answer is C. The professor offers to provide the student with the slides for the lecture when he says: "Why don't I just give you a copy of my PowerPoint slides for the lecture that you missed. Would that be helpful? "

8) The correct answer is A. This is a specific detail question. The professor explains that "it's a comprehensive test. So anything we have talked about in class can be included on the final exam".

9) The correct answer is C. This is another specific detail question. The professor states: "There was a 300-word personal response piece that's due next Tuesday".

10) The correct answer is B. This is another specific detail question. The professor tells the student: "If you can give me a note from your doctor as evidence of your medical condition, I can give you a two-week extension".

LISTENING PRACTICE TEST 1

SECTION 2 – LISTENING TEXT

Student: Hi, I was wondering if you could help me.

Staff: Well, I hope so . . . Have you got a question?

Student: Yeah, well, a problem is more like it!

Staff: Oh . . . That doesn't sound too good!

Student: The thing is . . . I'm living in Henderson Hall right now, but I'm wondering if it will be . . . if I could move to a different residential hall. I mean, I want to move immediately, if possible.

Staff: Um, that's kind of an unorthodox request. Not many students request to be moved in the middle of a term. And we usually don't consider any accommodation transfers until the beginning of a new semester, apart from compelling cases.

Student: What do you mean by "compelling cases"?

Staff: It just means that you have to have a really strong reason why you need to move immediately. Is there anything that makes your request to move more urgent?

Student: Well, it's really noisy. I can't study in my room. So I am finding it extremely frustrating . . . if I want to read, or write an essay or something.

Staff: Oh, I'm sorry, but that's just such a common complaint. I mean, we hear it all the time here at the accommodation office. And to be honest, that's why the library is open 24 hours . . . uh . . . we recommend that students study there.

Student: I see where you're going with this . . . It's just that Henderson Hall is quite far from the library. So I have to carry my laptop and all the books there, and of course, then I have to carry them back to my room again, which is very tiring.

Staff: Yes, but the library has a computer lab for students, so you wouldn't necessarily have to take your laptop, would you?

Student: Uh . . . the library has a computer lab . . . that's true . . . but it's usually completely full, and there aren't any free computers available.

Staff: Oh, that is a bit tricky.

Student: And, of course, it's so distracting in my room with all the loud music.

Staff: Have you tried speaking to your Resident Director about it?

Student: What's a "resident director"?

Staff: That's the person who lives in your hall of residence and who's in charge of day-to-day activities there, as well as complaints.

Student: Okay . . . so who's the Resident Director in charge of Henderson Hall?

Staff: Uh . . . let's have a look on my list . . . Let's see . . . here it is . . . It's John Marshall. I'm surprised you weren't introduced to him during your student orientation.

Student: That's my fault, I'm afraid. I missed orientation because I arrived on campus late. So we were never introduced.

Staff: Okay, well . . . that certainly clears up the mystery! I'd suggest that you have a talk with John. I mean, most halls of residence have set up "study hours", so if students don't keep the noise down during the quiet times that have been demarcated for studying, then the Resident Director can give the offending students three verbal warnings.

Student: Yeah, but I don't want the people I live with to know that I've complained about them.

Staff: No problem, it's a completely anonymous, confidential process.

Student: That's good to know. But . . . I mean . . . you're just talking about verbal warnings. What happens if the noisy students just keep ignoring the RD's warnings?

Staff: If they don't heed the warnings, then the RD files a formal complaint with us here at the Accommodation Office, and finally, we have the authority to remove the students.

Student: Oh, okay. I'll have a talk with John to get the ball rolling. Thanks so much for your help!

LISTENING PRACTICE TEST 1

SECTION 2 – ANSWERS AND EXPLANATIONS

11) The correct answer is "Henderson". The student says: "I'm living in Henderson Hall right now".

12) The correct answer is "move". The student says: I'm wondering if . . . I could *move* to a different residential hall".

13) The correct answer is "different". The student says: I'm wondering if . . . I could move to a *different* residential hall".

14) The correct answer is "no". This is a main idea question. The issue of the student's real need to move is present throughout the dialogue. The staff member suggests that the student's need is not compelling at several points in the conversation. For instance, she says: "Oh, I'm sorry, but that's just such a common complaint. I mean, we hear it all the time here at the accommodation office. And to be honest, that's why the library is open 24 hours . . . uh . . . we recommend that students study there".

15) The correct answer is "noisy". The student tells the staff member that "it's really noisy. I can't study in my room".

16) Possible correct answers are: read / write / study / concentrate. The student reiterates that he is having problems in his room when he says: "it's so distracting in my room with all the loud music".

17) The correct answer is "the library". The accommodation officer states: "The library is open 24 hours . . . we recommend that students study there".

18) The correct answer is "John Marshall". The student asks: "Who's the Resident Director in charge of Henderson Hall?" The staff member replies: "Let's have a look on my list . . . Let's see . . . here it is . . . It's John Marshall".

19) Possible correct answer are: arrived late / missed orientation. The accommodation officer remarks: "I'm surprised you weren't introduced to him [i.e., the resident director] during your student orientation". The student then responds: "That's my fault, I'm afraid. I missed orientation because I arrived on campus late. So we were never introduced".

20) The correct answer is "formal complaint". The accommodation officer explains that if noisy students "don't heed the warnings, then the RD files a formal complaint with us here at the Accommodation Office".

LISTENING PRACTICE TEST 1

SECTION 3 – LISTENING TEXT

Teacher: This afternoon, we'll be looking at the function of the human brain. We will also be talking about the way the function, as well as the dysfunction, of the human brain is measured. Now, as you may know, it was in 1929 that electrical activity in the human brain was first discovered. Hans Berger, the German psychiatrist who made the discovery, was despondent to find out, though, that his research was quickly dismissed by many other scientists.

The work of Berger was confirmed three years later, in 1932, when Edgar Adrian, a Briton, clearly demonstrated that the brain, like the heart, is profuse in its electrical activity. Because of Adrian's work, we know that the electrical impulses in the brain, called brain waves, are a mixture of four different frequencies. Here, I should say first of all that by "frequency", we are referring to the number of electrical impulses that occur in the brain per second.

Now . . . in order to measure brain activity and function, there are various types of equipment, which can perform various types of tests. For instance, we have traditionally used CAT and PET scans for this purpose. Okay, can anybody elucidate . . . between CAT and PET scans?

Student: Well . . . I'll take a stab at it. If I recall correctly, the PET scan works by means of an inert radioactive substance given to a patient, and this allows the doctor to observe the movement of the substance through the brain. As far as the CAT scan, well . . . they are like an X-ray of the brain, which is then displayed on a computer screen.

Teacher: Yes, that right. Now, can anybody talk about the differences between the appearances of CAT and PET scans?

Student: Oh, yeah . . . sorry . . . I should have talked about that, too. The PET scan shows up as one image, and that image will have different colours. And each one of the colours displays the pattern of the brain activity. With the CAT scan . . . that's a cross-section, so, unlike the PET scan, it can be viewed from different angles or positions. And of course, as far as patients are concerned, the CAT is far less invasive because they don't need to ingest a radioactive substance.

Teacher: Great . . . in addition to CAT and PET scan, we now have an MRI scan, which as you know works according to the principles of magnetism. The MRI is perhaps the most indispensable of all of the various scans due to its ability to map the brain in three dimensions.

LISTENING PRACTICE TEST 1

SECTION 3 – ANSWERS AND EXPLANATIONS

21) The correct answer is "brain". The teacher begins the seminar by stating that "This afternoon, we'll be looking at the function of the human brain".

22) The correct answer is "Berger". The teacher clearly mentions the name "Hans Berger" just after the start of the lecture.

23) Possible correct answers are: dismissed / disregarded. The teacher says: "Hans Berger, the German psychiatrist who made the discovery, was despondent to find out, though, that his research was quickly dismissed by many other scientists".

24) The correct answer is 1932. The teacher says: "The work of Berger was confirmed three years later, in 1932".

25) Possible correct answer are: Briton / British. The teacher identifies Adrian as follows: "Edgar Adrian, a Briton".

26) The correct answer is "frequencies". The teacher explains: "We know that the electrical impulses in the brain, called brain waves, are a mixture of four different frequencies".

27) The correct answer is "X-ray". The student responds to the teacher's question as follows: "As far as the CAT scan, well . . . they are like an X-ray of the brain, which is then displayed on a computer screen".

28) The correct answer is "PET". The student explains that "the PET scan works by means of an inert radioactive substance given to a patient".

29 and 30) The correct answers are A and C. The student explains that "With the CAT scan . . . that's a cross-section, so, unlike the PET scan, it can be viewed from different angles or positions. And of course, as far as patients are concerned, the CAT is far less invasive because they don't need to ingest a radioactive substance".

LISTENING PRACTICE TEST 1

SECTION 4 – LISTENING TEXT

Skyscrapers vary around the world from city to city, depending on local climate, conditions and, of course, terrain. This is especially true in the world's most heavily populated cities. No recent construction project exemplifies this more clearly than the building of the Hong Kong and Shanghai Bank Corporation (HSBC) in Hong Kong. So, in today's lecture, we're going to have a look at the construction of this particular high-rise building.

First of all, it is interesting to note that a very significant proportion of this structure was prefabricated. In other words, the building was designed so that it had many pre-built parts that were not constructed on site. This prefabrication made the project a truly international effort: The windows were manufactured in Austria, the exterior walls were fabricated in the United States, the toilets and air-conditioning were made in Japan, and many of the other components came from Germany. The prefabrication also had the advantage of making the construction more efficient, as well as minimising the intrusion and inconvenience to a great many people who continued to work in other buildings near the site.

The HSBC building consists of 47 storeys, which is an immense contrast to the twenty-story buildings in its vicinity. In fact, the previous buildings constructed on this site were limited by the soft and often waterlogged ground in the surrounding area. For this reason, the disruption of the ground water supply had to be carefully pondered prior to construction of the HSBC headquarters to ensure that subsidence, and potentially, collapse of the structure, could be averted.

Next, the concrete lower floor of the building was constructed so that work above ground could commence. During the next phase of construction, eight giant steel columns, which weighed more than a thousand tonnes, were erected to support the walls of the structure. In order to support the weight of the building, deep wells were sunk into the bedrock below the building, and then filled with concrete, to anchor each of the steel columns. To provide further support, steel beams stretch across the eight columns at five levels of the structure. Each of these steel beams comprises twin rectangular frames that are, in fact, two storeys high. Each steel beam also has hangers, which are used to support the floors.

Specially-designed cranes then lifted the prefabricated elements of the building into place. Most of the bank's exterior walls are taken up by large panes of window glass. The rest of the building is covered in aluminium panels. The external walls are also prefabricated in an aluminium finish that matched the rest of the building. So, when the external walls were finally lifted into position, they matched seamlessly with the rest of the building.

LISTENING PRACTICE TEST 1

SECTION 4 – ANSWERS AND EXPLANATIONS

31) The correct answer is "Hong Kong". The lecturer states: "the building of the Hong Kong and Shanghai Bank Corporation (HSBC) [is] in Hong Kong".

32) The correct answer is "United States". The lecturer tells us that "the exterior walls were fabricated in the United States".

33) The correct answer is "Germany". The lecturer adds that "many of the other components came from Germany".

34) The correct answer is "efficient". The speaker explains that "the prefabrication also had the advantage of making the construction more efficient".

35) The correct answer is 47. The lecturer says: "The HSBC building consists of 47 storeys".

36) The correct answer is "water". The lecturer explains that "the disruption of the ground water supply had to be carefully pondered prior to construction of the HSBC headquarters".

37) The correct answer is 1,000. The speaker says: "During the next phase of construction, eight giant steel columns, which weighed more than a thousand tonnes, were erected to support the walls of the structure".

38) The correct answer is "steel". The lecturer adds: "To provide further support, steel beams stretch across the eight columns at five levels of the structure".

39 and 40) The correct answers are "glass" and "aluminium". The lecturer finishes the talk by stating that "most of the bank's exterior walls are taken up by large panes of window glass. The rest of the building is covered in aluminium panels".

IELTS Practice Listening – Test 2
Answer Sheet

1. 21.
2. 22.
3. 23.
4. 24.
5. 25.
6. 26.
7. 27.
8. 28.
9. 29.
10. 30.
11. 31.
12. 32.
13. 33.
14. 34.
15. 35.
16. 36.
17. 37.
18. 38.
19. 39.
20. 40.

IELTS Practice Listening – Test 2

LISTENING PRACTICE TEST 2

SECTION 1   QUESTIONS 1 – 8

Choose the correct letter A, B or C.

1)   Why can't the student schedule an appointment for Friday?

  A. She can't come at 9:00 o'clock.

  B. The professor isn't available.

  C. She has a part-time job.

2)   What reason did the student give for being late to class?

  A. She has an earlier class that finishes late.

  B. She works part-time in the library.

  C. She takes her child to the day-care centre.

3)   What solution does the professor initially suggest?

  A. The student should stop going to the day-care centre.

  B. The student should leave her daughter off early.

  C. The student should go to the day-care centre after class.

4)   Why does the student reject the professor's initial suggestion?

  A. The day-care centre doesn't have any available staff.

  B. The day-care centre can't legally open before 9:00.

  C. The day-care centre doesn't have a licence.

Continued on next page.

5) What information does the student miss because she is late to class?
   A. note taking
   B. answers to exercises
   C. the refresher session

6) Why is the student's tardiness inconvenient for her classmates?
   A. They have to tell her what she has missed.
   B. They have to begin the class again.
   C. They have to wait while the professor repeats the information.

7) Why does the professor mention the student who attends the 2:00 o'clock class?
   A. to give an example about working part time
   B. to show that the 9:00 o'clock class is inconvenient
   C. to suggest that the students swap places

8) How will the student know what to do next?
   A. The professor will email her.
   B. She will need to speak to the professor.
   C. She will need to talk to the student in the 2:00 o'clock class.

SECTION 2   QUESTIONS 9 – 18

Questions 9-16

Complete the chart below, using **ONLY ONE WORD** in each gap.

Century	Music influenced by:	Musical Type or Genre	Comments
Prior to 13th century	Chant	Monophonic	"Mono" means one thing **9)** _____ or by itself.
15th century	Renaissance	Polyphonic	Combines notes from **10)** _____ sources.
16th century	Greek **11)** _____	Opera	Especially pronounced in the **12)** _____ opera.
17th century	Proliferation of musical **13)** _____	Sinfonias / Concertos	Arrangements for instruments such as **14)** _____ and organ.
18th century	**15)** _____ - born composers: Bach and Handel	Oratorio / Liturgical	Predominance of stringed instruments, especially the **16)** _____ .

Questions 17-18: Choose 2 letters from A – E below that the speaker mentions about Beethoven in the last part of the listening passage.

Beethoven made a significant contribution to 18th century music because:

A. He removed the need for aesthetics in music.

B. His work established the beginning of the classical period.

C. He contributed to many styles of music.

D. He simplified the style of symphony music.

E. His work bridged the romantic and classical periods.

SECTION 3   QUESTIONS 19 – 28

Questions 19-28

Choose the correct letters A, B, C, D or E.

19) What is the main idea of this discussion?
    A. reasons for teenage experimental smoking
    B. recent trends in teenage smoking
    C. teenage smoking and peer pressure

20) What do current statistics on teenage smoking reveal?
    A. The rate of teenage smoking is greater than that for adults.
    B. The rate of teenage smoking is less than that for adults.
    C. The rate of teenage smoking is unchanged compared to that for adults.

21-22) *For this question only,* **CHOOSE TWO ANSWERS**.
    What two reasons are given for the increase in teenage smoking?
    A. the decrease in the price of cigarettes
    B. feelings of alienation from the family
    C. lawsuits against tobacco companies
    D. disadvantaged home life
    E. peer pressure

Continued on next page.

23) What does the professor mean when he says: "You hit the nail on the head"?

   A. The student's remarks were very appropriate.

   B. The student has touched on a sensitive subject.

   C. The student needs to focus on the main points.

24) The rise in teenage smoking in the early 1900s:

   A. took place because parents were working.

   B. occurred in disadvantaged homes.

   C. was predominantly in youth from affluent families.

25) From the discussion, what statement about lawsuits against tobacco companies can be surmised?

   A. They affected teenagers more than adults.

   B. Cigarette companies had to increase their prices because of the expense of hiring lawyers.

   C. Cigarette companies had to reduce their prices to increase demand.

26) The price of cigarettes

   A. is not a factor in smoking by teens.

   B. causes an increase in smoking by teens.

   C. causes a decrease in smoking by teens.

Continued on next page.

27) What is the outcome of teenage experimental smoking?

   A. Most experimental smokers do not manage to quit.

   B. It causes an increase in cigarette prices.

   C. It can lead to drug addiction.

28) How does the teacher support his comments about experimental smoking?

   A. By citing a medical authority

   B. By giving statistical data

   C. By mentioning general information

SECTION 4   QUESTIONS 29 – 40

*Complete the notes below. Write **ONLY ONE WORD OR NUMBER** in each gap.*

Lecture Topic: Genetic **29)** _____

Part 1 – Definitions and Examples

Definition: the impact of genetics on how a plant or animal

30) _____

Examples: Cereals and **31)** _____ or **32)** _____

Part 2 – DNA

DNA – Genetic **33)** _____ of organisms are found in DNA.

DNA consists of **34)** _____ separate components called nucleotides.

DNA chain provides **35)** _____ information for cells.

Example: Can be used to detect diseases like **36)** _____ or Alzheimer's disease

PART 3 – Gene splicing

Gene splicing – cutting DNA from one organism and **37)** _____ into another organism.

Example: The super **38)** _____ uses DNA from cold-water

39) _____

Example: Factor **40)** _____ is a genetic agent in blood.

ANSWER KEY – LISTENING PRACTICE TEST 2

1) C

2) C

3) B

4) B

5) C

6) A

7) C

8) A

9) alone

10) different (various is also acceptable)

11) drama

12) Italian

13) instruments

14) piano

15) German

16) violin

17-18) C, E

19) B

20) A

21-22) B, E

23) A

24) C

25) C

26) A

27) A

28) B

29) engineering

30) behaves

31-32) fruit, vegetables

33) characteristics

34) 4

35) reproductive

36) cancer

37) inserting

38) tomato

39) fish

40) 9

TEXTS, ANSWERS AND EXPLANATIONS

LISTENING PRACTICE TEST 2

SECTION 1 – LISTENING TEXT

Student: Hi Professor Johnson. Have you got a minute?

Teacher: Uh . . . well . . . I have a class in about five minutes. Is it a quick question, or would you like to schedule an appointment during my office hour on Friday?

Student: Oh . . . well . . . I'm afraid I can't come on Friday because I work in the library part-time. Anyway, hopefully it won't take too long.

Teacher: Okay. What's up?

Student: Well, you've probably noticed that I'm usually late for your 9:00 class.

Teacher: Yes, of course I have, and to be honest, I'm glad you've dropped in to talk about that.

Student: The thing is . . . you know . . . I'm a mature student . . . and I'm a single parent too . . . I have a little girl . . . she's four. I have to drop her off at the day-care centre before class. Well . . . the day-care centre only opens at 9:00, so that's why I'm always late, because I have to go there first.

Teacher: Well, have you talked to the people who run the day-care centre? Would it be possible to drop your little girl off a little bit early? I mean one of their members of staff could be available before 9:00.

Student: No, I'm afraid not. I already asked them that, and the person in charge told me that because of their licence, they can't open before 9:00. It's something to do with the regulations of running a day-care centre, and it just can't be changed.

Teacher: Oh, I see. That's too bad. It must be inconvenient for you, but you know it's also causing inconvenience . . . in a way . . . to the other students in the 9:00 class.

Student: Uh . . . I'm not really with you.

Teacher: Well, what I'm getting at is . . . your persistent tardiness . . . it's become a little disruptive. I mean . . . I'm sure you've noticed that we usually start the class off with questions and a "refresher" session from the previous class, so you miss all of that information. And then, of course, you have to get another one of the students to repeat all the information to you, and that's where the inconvenience comes in for them, in a way.

Student: Well . . . what do you think I can do? I mean . . . I'm sorry, but it's just not going to be possible for me to be there on time.

Teacher: Okay . . . look . . . there is a student in the same course, but that class meets at 2:00 o'clock. She can't come then because she has a part-time job, so if it's okay with you, maybe the two of you could change places. She could come to the 9:00 o'clock and you could take her place in the 2:00 o'clock session.

Student: Oh, yes! That would be great. It would really solve my problem.

Teacher: Okay . . . well . . . leave it with me . . . I'll talk to the other student and see if she'll agree to joining the 9:00 o'clock group. Then, I'll send you an email to let you know. Is that okay?

Student: That's great. Thanks a lot, Professor Johnson. I really appreciate it! See you later.

LISTENING PRACTICE TEST 2

SECTION 1 – ANSWERS AND EXPLANATIONS

1) The correct answer is C. The student can't schedule an appointment for Friday because she has a part-time job. She says: "I'm afraid I can't come on Friday because I work in the library part-time".

2) The correct answer is C. The reason that the student gave for being late to class is that she takes her child to the day-care centre. She tells the professor: "The day-care centre only opens at 9:00, so that's why I'm always late, because I have to go there first".

3) The correct answer is B. The professor initially suggests that the student should leave her daughter off early. He asks the student: "Would it be possible to drop your little girl off a little bit early? I mean one of their members of staff could be available before 9:00".

4) The correct answer is B. The student rejects the professor's initial suggestion because the day-care centre can't legally open before 9:00. She explains to the professor that "I already asked them that, and the person in charge told me that because of their licence, they can't open before 9:00".

5) The correct answer is C. The student misses the refresher session because she is late for class. The professor says: "I'm sure you've noticed that we usually start off the class with questions and a 'refresher' session from the previous class, so you miss all of that information".

6) The correct answer is A. The student's tardiness is inconvenient for her classmates because they have to tell her what she has missed. The professor explains that "you have to get another one of the students to repeat all of that information to you, and that's where the inconvenience comes in for them, in a way".

7) The correct answer is C. The professor mentions the student who attends the 2:00 o'clock class to suggest that the students swap places. The professor says: "There is a student in the same course, but that class meets at 2:00 o'clock. She can't come then because she just got a part-time job, so if it's okay with you, maybe the two of you could change places. She could come to the 9:00 o'clock and you could take her place in the 2:00 o'clock session".

8) The correct answer is A. The professor will email the student to tell her what to do next. He says: "Leave it with me . . . I'll talk to the other student and see if she'll agree to joining the 9:00 o'clock group. Then, I'll send you an email to let you know".

LISTENING PRACTICE TEST 2

SECTION 2 – LISTENING TEXT

The tradition of music in the western world – in other words, music as we know it today – originated in the genre of chanting. Prior to the thirteenth century, chant was the dominant mode of music. Notably, chanting was a monophonic form of music. Monophonic, let's have a look at that word . . . "mono" is from a Greek word. It means one thing alone or by itself. "Phonic" is also Greek in origin – and it means sound. So, monophonic music consists of only one sound or voice that is combined various notes in a series.

Polyphonic music appeared in the fifteenth century during the early Renaissance period. In contrast to monophonic music, polyphonic music consists of more than one voice or instrument, and it combines the notes from the different sources together simultaneously. As polyphony developed, musical traditions began to change, and this meant that music began to rely on a greater range of voices. And really this was a big range . . . um . . . I mean . . . from the very high to the very low. This kind of polyphonic musical influence is also present in the national anthems that emerged in various countries during this era.

Next, let's have a look at the sixteenth century. Particularly . . . especially during the end of the sixteenth century, there was an attempt to return to the tradition of Greek drama. This had a particular influence on the opera. As a result, the opera expanded to include oratorios, which are extended sung musical compositions on a particular subject. This phenomenon was especially pronounced in the Italian opera, and so, the opera, in turn, dominated the musical style of the early seventeenth century.

The seventeenth century also witnessed the proliferation of musical instruments. Musical compositions and arrangements for keyboard instruments, such as the piano and organ, thrived during this period. Music for the orchestra, arrangements like sinfonias and concertos, also began to take off during this time.

Next, let's look at the eighteenth century. The eighteenth century was marked by the development of baroque music. Stringed instruments, particularly the violin, were predominant throughout this epoch. Since many of the German-born composers studied abroad, baroque music was regarded to possess an international style. Other forms of classical music, especially the symphony, also developed during this century.

Okay, so, eighteenth century music – many people believe this anyway – was dominated by two German-born geniuses: Bach and Handel. These two composers wrote music in almost every genre, including opera and oratorio music. Handel, of course, studied in both Italy and England, bearing out the point I made earlier about the international flavour of the musical compositions of this century. Bach, while similar in many ways to Handel, is perhaps best known for his liturgical – and by this I mean religious – music. Some music history scholars point out that Bach's work is significant historically, too, since it shows the pervasive impact of the Reformation on the musical style of this century.

Finally, then, no lecture on musical genre would be complete without a discussion of Beethoven. Beethoven really was a remarkable and versatile musician. He contributed to almost every style of music during this era, including piano, strings and symphonies, and he also expanded the form of the symphony to include greater orchestration. Beethoven is often seen as the crucial link between the classical and romantic periods. He added deeper texture – by this I mean the depth and breadth of different kinds of musical sound – as well as aesthetics – and here by aesthetics we are talking about the beauty of the music itself, in other words, the sheer pleasure or enjoyment that a person can receive from listening to a truly beautifully composed piece of music. For these reasons, the music of Beethoven is commonly regarded as establishing the end of the classical period.

LISTENING PRACTICE TEST 2

SECTION 2 – ANSWERS AND EXPLANATIONS

9) The correct answer is "alone". The speaker says: "Now, monophonic, let's have a look at that word . . . 'mono' is from a Greek word. It means one thing *alone* or by itself".

10) The correct answer is "different". The lecturer explains that "polyphonic music consists of more than one voice or instrument, and it combines the notes from the *different* sources together".

11) The correct answer is "drama". The speaker says: "let's have a look at the sixteenth century . . . especially during the end of the sixteenth century, there was an attempt to return to the tradition of Greek drama".

12) The correct answer is "Italian". The lecturer explains: "This phenomenon was especially pronounced in the Italian opera".

13) The correct answer is "instruments". The speaker says: "The seventeenth century also witnessed the proliferation of musical instruments".

14) The correct answer is "piano". The lecturer explains: "Musical compositions and arrangements for keyboard instruments, such as the piano and organ, thrived during this period".

15) The correct answer is "German". The speaker says: "Eighteenth century music – many people believe this anyway – was dominated by two German-born geniuses: Bach and Handel".

16) The correct answer is "violin". The lecturer explains: "Stringed instruments, particularly the violin, were predominant throughout this epoch".

17-18) The correct answers are C and E. Beethoven made a significant contribution to 18th century music because: (C) He contributed to many styles of music; and (E) His work bridged the romantic and classical periods. The speaker says: "Beethoven really was a remarkable and versatile musician. He contributed to almost every style of music during his era . . . Beethoven is often seen as the crucial link between the classical and romantic periods".

LISTENING PRACTICE TEST 2

SECTION 3 – LISTENING TEXT

TEACHER: In today's class, we're going to talk about a worrying sociological problem, that of teenage smoking. Although the trends show that smoking by adults has been declining steadily over the past few decades, the percentage of teenagers who smoke only started to drop in the late 1990s. In fact, the current statistics on this are really quite alarming because, at present, the rate of teenagers who smoke is nearly 50 percent greater than the rate for adult smokers. So, my first question is this: what reasons can you give for these trends?

STUDENT: Well, could it be that teenagers are more prone to pressure from their friends, you know, peer pressure, and so of course they want to fit in with their social group and smoking is one way to do that.

TEACHER: Yes, good answer! Peer pressure is really one of the biggest reasons why teens smoke. But, you know, peer pressure has always existed from time immemorial. Can you think of any other reasons . . . um . . . I mean reasons that are specifically connected with the current social and cultural phenomena?

STUDENT: Oh, yeah, I see what you're getting at. You know, with the increase in the use of things like the Internet and with a lot of parents working long hours, maybe kids feel a bit . . . sort of . . . alienated . . . is that the right word? I mean, like if the kid is by himself a lot maybe he's just going to feel alone and not connected to anybody else but his friends and then of course he's more susceptible to fall into the trap of smoking because of peer pressure.

TEACHER: Yes, exactly! You hit the nail on the head! In fact, recent research shows that the rise in teenage smoking in the 1990s primarily took place in the youth from more affluent families – earning good incomes. So of course children were not from disadvantaged homes as some sociologists would like us to believe . . . quite the opposite . . . the most striking and precipitous rise was in teenagers with the most financially advantageous backgrounds.

And we know that because of various law suits against the major tobacco companies . . . the price of cigarettes actually declined sharply in the 1990s, which of course added fuel to the fire that was already burning in this area socially. What I mean is, paradoxically, these teenagers were from well-off families and could have afforded to pay the higher prices, yet contrary to these market forces, the price of tobacco products was reduced during this time.

Okay . . . so from this we can surmise that the price doesn't really appear to be a factor in smoking by teens. Probably, this is because teenagers often view themselves as "experimental smokers". Now, that's an interesting term . . . "experimental smokers" . . . what do you think it means or implies?

STUDENT: It means they see their own smoking behaviour as an experiment, obviously. So what that implies . . . I suppose . . . is . . . well . . . these kids think they are just trying it out, so they aren't necessarily . . . actually . . . going to do it . . . I mean smoke . . . for their lifetime . . . They maybe just view it as something they can try and then stop doing it later.

TEACHER: Yes, I couldn't have said it better myself! Okay . . . So, the next logical question is: Do you think that most of these teenagers . . . these experimental smokers . . . will eventually manage to stop smoking?

STUDENT: Personally, I think that's highly unlikely. Quitting smoking is an extremely difficult thing to do . . . I've heard it can even be tougher than beating drug addiction . . . because the nicotine in cigarettes is very highly addictive itself.

TEACHER: Yes, that's absolutely right. And, again, the statistics bear this out. 56 percent of all the students who smoked predicted that they would not still be smokers after five years of graduation. But when the data was gathered five years later, only 31 percent of them had actually quit smoking.

LISTENING PRACTICE TEST 2

SECTION 3 – ANSWERS AND EXPLANATIONS

19) The correct answer is B. The main idea of this discussion is recent trends in teenage smoking. We know this because the teacher begins the seminar as follows: "In today's class, we're going to talk about a worrying sociological problem, that of teenage smoking. Although the trends show that smoking by adults has been declining steadily over the past few decades, the percentage of teenagers who smoke only started to drop in the late 1990s".

20) The correct answer is A. Current statistics on teenage smoking reveal that the rate of teenage smoking is greater than that for adults. The teacher says: "The rate of teenagers who smoke is nearly 50 percent greater than the rate for adult smokers".

21-22) The correct answers are B and E. The two reasons given for the increase in teenage smoking are (B) feelings of alienation from within the family; and (E) peer pressure. The student says: "Teenagers are more prone to pressure from their friends, you know, peer pressure, and so of course they want to fit in with their social group and smoking is one way to do that." The student later adds: "You know, with the increase in the use of things like the Internet and with a lot of parents working long hours, maybe kids feel a bit . . . sort of . . . alienated".

23) The correct answer is A. When the teacher says: "You hit the nail on the head", he means that the student's remarks were very appropriate. We know this because the teacher exclaims: "Yes, exactly!"

24) The correct answer is C. The rise in teenage smoking in the early 1900s was predominantly in youth from affluent families. The teacher comments that "the rise in teenage smoking in the 1990s primarily took place in the youth from more affluent families – earning good incomes".

25) The correct answer is C. Cigarette companies had to reduce their prices to increase demand because of lawsuits against tobacco companies. The teacher explains this phenomenon as follows: "And we know that because of various law suits against the major tobacco companies . . . the price of cigarettes actually declined sharply in the early 1990s, which of course added fuel to the fire that was already burning in this area socially. What I mean is, paradoxically, these teenagers were from well-off families and could have afforded to pay the higher prices, yet contrary to these market forces, the price of tobacco products was reduced during this time".

26) The correct answer is A. The price of cigarettes is not a factor in smoking by teens. The teacher says: "We can surmise that price doesn't really appear to be a factor in smoking by teens".

27) The correct answer is A. The outcome of teenage experimental smoking is that most experimental smokers do not manage to quit. The teacher asks: "Do you think that most of these teenagers . . . these experimental smokers . . . will eventually manage to stop smoking?" The student correctly responds: "Personally, I think that's highly unlikely. Quitting smoking is an extremely difficult thing to do . . . I've heard it can even be tougher than beating drug addiction . . . because the nicotine in cigarettes is very highly addictive itself".

28) The correct answer is B. The teacher supports his comments about experimental smoking by giving statistical data. He states that "56 percent of all the students who smoked predicted that they would not still be smokers after five years of graduation. But when the data was gathered five years later, only 31 percent of them had actually quit smoking".

LISTENING PRACTICE TEST 2

SECTION 4 – LISTENING TEXT

Okay everybody, I think we should probably get started. In the lecture for today, we're going to take a look at a hotly-debated and contentious topic: genetic engineering. So, first of all, we'll go into a little bit of the background information about this topic. And then we'll move on to consider the nuts and bolts . . . and by that I mean the basis of . . . the genetic aspects of genetic engineering. And finally, we'll have a look at why this topic has become such a thorny issue recently.

Okay . . . Genetic engineering . . . now as biology students you'll know that this term refers to the process of re-programming the genetic materials that dictate how a plant or animal behaves. And it's probably no surprise to you that scientists have been conducting genetic engineering on plants for quite a few years now . . . things like cereals and fruit, for example. Now, this has been done to produce better fruit . . . to grow fruit . . . or even vegetables, for that matter . . . outside of their normal season, and to make other plants, especially cereal crops, more resistant to damage from insects and disease. So, of course, the next question is . . . all may be aware of the basic idea behind genetic engineering, but what I'm exactly

. . . um . . . I'm referring to is . . . how is genetic engineering carried out on a genetic or biological level specifically and precisely? . . . That's the question we'll look at.

Well, as we all know, the genetic characteristics of any organism are present in its DNA . . . DNA . . . um . . . I don't need to write that on the board, do I? . . . um . . . DNA . . . is the genetic material found in each and every living cell. These form a genetic code and are formed from long molecules . . . like chains . . . and these DNA chains consist of four separate components called nucleotides . . . okay . . . that's a bit . . . bit of a difficult term . . . I'd better put that one on the board . . . nucleotides . . .

It's the order of these nucleotides on the DNA chain that determines the reproductive information for the cells. In other words, the specific genetic information along any point of this DNA chain will determine a particular gene . . . genetic trait. By way of example . . . in the case of human beings . . . a particular portion of your DNA might show your doctor if you are susceptible to a disease, like cancer or Alzheimer's disease.

So, then, in order to carry out what is known as genetic engineering, gene splicing needs to be done at first. This describes the process whereby a small part of the DNA chain for one characteristic of one organism is cut out of the DNA chain for that organism and inserted into the DNA chain of another organism from another species.

This has produced results like the "super-tomato". Now, the "super-tomato" was genetically engineered by inserting some DNA from cold-water fish . . . the particular gene resistance to cold temperatures was isolated on the DNA chain of the fish and was removed. This cold-resistant gene was re-inserted into an ordinary tomato plant . . . and lo and behold . . . we've now got tomato plants that can grow in cold weather conditions.

Another experiment that was even more notorious was Factor 9. Factor 9 is a genetic agent that is responsible for the clotting of blood. So if some people have a birth defect and are born without Factor 9 in their DNA chain, it would be really easy for them to bleed to death in the event of an accident.

LISTENING PRACTICE TEST 2

SECTION 4 – ANSWERS AND EXPLANATIONS

29) The correct answer is "engineering". The lecturer begins his talk as follows: "In the lecture for today, we're going to take a look at a hotly-debated and contentious topic: genetic *engineering*".

30) The correct answer is "behaves". The lecturer says: "Genetic engineering . . . now as biology students you'll know that this term refers to the process of re-programming the genetic materials that dictate how a plant or animal *behaves*".

31-32) The correct answers are "fruit" and "vegetables". The lecturer comments: "Scientists have been conducting genetic engineering on plants for quite a few years now . . . things like cereals and *fruit*, for example. Now, this has been done to produce better fruit . . . to grow fruit . . . or even *vegetables*, for that matter . . . outside of their normal season".

33) The correct answer is "characteristics". The lecturer says: "The genetic *characteristics* of any organism are present in its DNA.

34) The correct answer is 4. The lecturer explains that "DNA chains consist of *four* separate components called nucleotides".

35) The correct answer is "reproductive". The lecturer says: "It's the order of these nucleotides on the DNA chain that determines the reproductive information for the cells".

36) The correct answer is "cancer". The lecturer explains that "a particular portion of your DNA might show your doctor if you are susceptible to a disease, like *cancer* or Alzheimer's disease".

37) The correct answer is "inserting". The lecturer says: "Gene splicing . . . this describes the process whereby a small part of the DNA chain for one characteristic of one organism is cut out of the DNA chain for that organism and *inserted* into the DNA chain of another organism from another species". Note that you must change the form of the verb from –ed to –ing in order to make it grammatically correct.

38) The correct answer is "tomato". The lecturer says: "The 'super-*tomato*' was genetically engineered by inserting some DNA from cold-water fish".

39) The correct answer is "fish". The lecturer says: "The 'super-tomato' was genetically engineered by inserting some DNA from cold-water *fish*".

40) The correct answer is 9. The lecturer says: "Factor *9* is a genetic agent that is responsible for the clotting of blood".

IELTS Practice Listening – Test 3
Answer Sheet

1.   21.
2.   22.
3.   23.
4.   24.
5.   25.
6.   26.
7.   27.
8.   28.
9.   29.
10.   30.
11.   31.
12.   32.
13.   33.
14.   34.
15.   35.
16.   36.
17.   37.
18.   38.
19.   39.
20.   40.

© COPYRIGHT 1995, 2014, 2021. IELTS Success Associates dba www.examsam.com
This material may not be copied or reproduced in any form.

IELTS Practice Listening – Test 3

LISTENING PRACTICE TEST 3

SECTION 1   **QUESTIONS 1 – 8**

Choose the correct letter A, B or C.

1) What problem is the student experiencing?
    A. He forgot his password.
    B. He is unable to log in.
    C. He wasn't able to register.

2) What does the student mean when he says, "I know them by heart"?
    A. He has memorised his ID and password.
    B. He understands that the ID and password are necessary.
    C. He has written down the ID and password.

3) What specifically does the error message state?
    A. unable to process
    B. no log on
    C. invalid password characters

Continued on next page.

4) According to the computer assistant, what mistake do students often make when creating a new password?
   A. They create invalid messages.
   B. They forget to include certain required characters.
   C. They try to use forbidden symbols.

5) On what page of the student handbook are the computer rules provided?
   A. 29
   B. 30
   C. 39

6) What comment does the student make about his handbook?
   A. It was too difficult to read.
   B. He didn't feel like reading it.
   C. He never received one.

7) How does the computer assistant attempt to solve the student's problem?
   A. By giving a detailed step-by-step explanation.
   B. By describing common problems all students face.
   C. By referring the student to another university department

8) What is the outcome at the end of the conversation?
   A. The student has to go to Computer Services to obtain a new password.
   B. The student manages to log in to the computer system successfully.
   C. The computer assistant changes the student's password.

SECTION 2   QUESTIONS 9 – 19

Questions 9-16

Complete the chart below, using **ONLY ONE WORD** in each gap.

Food Group	Examples	Comments
9) _____	potatoes, bread and 10) _____	Supply 11) _____ to the body
Fruit and 12) _____	apples	Necessary to eat a 13) _____ of food from this group. 14) _____ portions recommended each day.
Protein	meat, fish and 15) _____ products	Limit intake of red meat, cheese and 16) _____

Questions 17-19

Choose the correct letter A, B or C.

17) Sugar consumption
    A. poses no health risk.
    B. should be totally avoided.
    C. should be limited.

18) How does the teacher support his statement about food additives and chemicals?
    A. By giving reasons for their dangers.
    B. By describing the public's general preference.
    C. By discussing a specific medical case study.

19) Which one of the following statements is correct according to the discussion?
    A. Healthy nutrition means that food is consumed from five major groups.
    B. Processed and convenience foods may damage the health.
    C. Energy requirements remain constant regardless of a person's age.

SECTION 3   QUESTIONS 20 – 29

Questions 20-22

Complete each sentence, using **NO MORE THAN THREE WORDS**.

20) The name of the education model is being discussed is . . . .

21) Students function at different . . . .

22) Students in the "comfort zone" are at the . . . .

Questions 23-29

Choose the correct letter A, B or C.

23) How does the teacher support her statement that "student readiness is not a static entity"?
   A. By discussing the needs of above-average students
   B. By explaining the ways in which a student's level can change
   C. By citing data and statistics

Continued on next page.

24) What does the teacher state about curriculum design?
   A. It is the duty of the teachers to decide which design is best.
   B. Teachers usually disagree about the curriculum.
   C. It is especially important for below-average students.

25) Which one of the following is the best description of the "question adjustment" strategy?
   A. The teacher should mainly ask easy questions to build student confidence.
   B. The teacher should ask questions at various levels of difficulty.
   C. The teacher should ask each individual student a different question.

26) What learning materials can be used in question adjustment?
   A. posters
   B. quizzes
   C. tests

27) Why is formal assessment given to students?
   A. It counts for a mark.
   B. It challenges the students.
   C. It stretches capable students.

28) What is the purpose of informal assessment?
   A. to determine student readiness
   B. to administer tests
   C. to build student confidence

Continued on next page.

29) Which one of the following statements is correct according to the discussion?
    A. Students prefer informal assessment.
    B. Students will only be confident when they have a low level of readiness.
    C. Student confidence enhances student readiness.

SECTION 4   QUESTIONS 30 – 40

Questions 30-34

Complete the chart below. Write **ONLY ONE WORD OR NUMBER** in each gap.

Explorer	Years	Achievement
Ernest Shakleton	1907-1909	Travelled across the Transantarctic **30)** _____
Roald Amundsen	1911	First to reach the **31)** _____ South Pole
Richard Evelyn Byrd	1930s & **32)** _____	Implemented land **33)** _____
Rear Admiral Dufek	1956	Landed an **34)** _____

Continued on next page.

Questions 35-37

Choose the correct letter A, B or C.

35) What causes atrophy of the Antarctic ice sheet?
   A. rain
   B. frost
   C. melting

36) Both methods used to measure the size of the ice sheet
   A. require satellite technology.
   B. may result in errors.
   C. calculate new precipitation.

37) Measurement of the ice sheet is important because of
   A. fossil fuel reliance.
   B. global warming.
   C. volcanic eruptions.

Continued on next page.

Questions 38-40

38-40) Which of the following statements give the main ideas from the talk?

CHOOSE THREE LETTERS.

A. Ernest Shackleton was the first to explore Antarctica.

B. There have been several important expeditions to the Antarctic in the twentieth and twenty-first centuries.

C. The expeditions to the Antarctic have resulted in many important scientific discoveries.

D. The Antarctic ice sheet constantly shrinks and expands.

E. Scientific discoveries about the Antarctic help us to understand the world's ecosphere.

ANSWER KEY – LISTENING PRACTICE TEST 3

1) B

2) A

3) C

4) C

5) C

6) B

7) A

8) B

9) carbohydrate

10) cereals

11) energy

12) vegetables

13) variety

14) 5

15) dairy

16) cream

17) C

18) A

19) B

20) student readiness model

21) levels of ability

22) optimum learning level

23) B

24) A

25) B

26) A

27) A

28) C

29) C

30) mountains

31) geographic

32) 1940 / 1940s

33) transport

34) aeroplane

35) C

36) B

37) B

38-40) B, C, E

TEXTS, ANSWERS AND EXPLANATIONS

LISTENING PRACTICE TEST 3

SECTION 1 – LISTENING TEXT

Student: Hi. I was wondering if you could help me.

Staff: Well . . . Let's see . . . what's your question?

Student: Well, I just registered for classes on Thursday last week, and I received my computer ID and password yesterday, but when I try to log in to the computer system on campus, I keep getting an error message.

Staff: Oh . . . okay . . . do you remember what the message says?

Student: No . . . unfortunately, I don't . . . It just gives me a message saying that I can't log in.

Staff: Have you got your ID and password with you?

Student: No, but I know them by heart.

Staff: Okay, great! Uh . . . Why don't you try to log on to this computer right here, and we'll see what happens.

Student: Okay. Here goes . . . There . . . the message I keep getting. Do you see it? It says something about invalid password characters.

Staff: Right . . . that's a common problem students experience. You see, there are certain characters and symbols that you can't use in your password . . . things like the slash, the question mark, and the number sign, for example.

Student: Why's that?

Staff: Those kinds of symbols are forbidden for passwords because the computer uses them in mathematical calculations. Have you tried to use any symbol like that in your password?

Student: Yeah, I have, but I didn't realise that I wasn't supposed to.

Staff: Well . . . it's all explained on page 39 in your student handbook . . . so . . .

Student: Oh . . . right . . . I get it . . . It was my responsibility to read that, but you know, I was just so tired after I had registered that I didn't really have the energy to read the handbook all the way through.

Staff: No problem. Actually, we're used to that . . . I mean we hear that a lot.

Student: So, what can we do now to solve the problem?

Staff: It should be pretty easy to solve, actually. Uh . . . you just need to press control-alt-delete, and the system will ask you to change your password. So then you should type in a new one that doesn't have one of those forbidden characters in it. If course, I'm sure I don't need to remind you to choose a password that you can remember!

Student: Can I try to change it now and see what happens?

Staff: Please do. That's a good idea.

Student: Okay . . . let me try this . . . okay . . . I put the new one in now. The system seems to have accepted it. Can I try logging again?

Staff: Yes, go ahead.

Student: Okay . . . there's my ID now . . . the new password . . . Great! I'm in! Thanks so much for your help!

LISTENING PRACTICE TEST 3

SECTION 1 – ANSWERS AND EXPLANATIONS

1) The correct answer is B. The student is unable to log in to the computer. He says: "I received my computer ID and password yesterday, but when I try to log in to the computer system on campus, I keep getting an error message".

2) The correct answer is A. When student says, "I know them by heart", he means that he has memorised his ID and password. We know this because he says he doesn't have the password with him, but then he is able to enter them into the system anyway.

3) The correct answer is C. The error message states that there are invalid password characters. The student says: "There . . . the message I keep getting. Do you see it? It says something about invalid password characters".

4) The correct answer is C. According to the computer assistant, students often make the mistake of trying to use forbidden symbols when creating a new password. The assistant says: "There are certain characters and symbols that you can't use in your password . . . things like the slash, the question mark, and the number sign, for example".

5) The correct answer is C. The assistant states that "it's all explained on page 39 in your student handbook".

6) The correct answer is B. The student implies that he didn't feel like reading his handbook. He says: "Oh . . . right . . . I get it . . . It was my responsibility to read that, but you know, I was just so tired after I had registered that I didn't really have the energy to read the handbook all the way through".

7) The correct answer is A. The computer assistant attempts to solve the student's problem by giving a detailed step-by-step explanation. She gives the following steps: "You just need to press control-alt-delete, and the system will ask you to change your password. So then you should type in a new one that doesn't have one of those forbidden characters in it. If course, I'm sure I don't need to remind you to choose a password that you can remember!"

8) The correct answer is B. The outcome at the end of the conversation is that the student manages to log in to the computer system successfully. He exclaims: "Great! I'm in! Thanks so much for your help!"

LISTENING PRACTICE TEST 3

SECTION 2 – LISTENING TEXT

TEACHER: So today, we're going to talk about good nutrition. Now, everybody knows that good nutrition is essential for good health. Indeed, a healthy diet can help a person to maintain a good body weight, promote mental wellbeing and even reduce . . . reduce the risk of disease. So, first of all today, we are going to look at the answer to the question: What does healthy nutrition consist of?

Well, really, a healthy diet should include food from four major groups. These four groups are carbohydrate, fruit, vegetables and protein. The first of the four groups, carbohydrate, includes food like potatoes, bread and cereals. Although carbohydrates seem to have got bad press lately, in fact, they are an essential part of healthy nutrition. They provide the building blocks for supplying energy to the body.

The second and third food groups are fruit and vegetables – although some people would just include these as one group. This may be easy to understand at first blush, but it is worth pointing out that good nutrition depends on eating a variety of fruit and vegetables. While the old adage "An apple a day keeps the doctor away" may appear to be sound advice, eating the same fruit or vegetables daily . . . it's really not the best advice in reality. The amount of fruit and vegetables . . . that's also important to bear in mind. Most medical practitioners in the United States now recommend a minimum consumption of 5 portions of fruit or vegetables every day.

Now . . . protein includes food such as meat and fish, as well as dairy products, like milk and cheese. However, lean protein is better than fatty protein, so it's best to limit the consumption of red meat, rich cheeses and cream. In addition to keeping an eye on fat intake, the amount of sugar a person eats should also be moderated. I want to ask as this point, do you think that it's better to give up sugar completely in order to achieve optimal health?

STUDENT: Um . . . I don't think a person should try to forego sweets altogether. It's just that consuming too much sugar is . . . is often connected to health problems later in life, like Type II diabetes, so I think the thing is . . . uh . . . to try to be careful not to eat too much sugar.

TEACHER: Yes, that's right. Like the old saying goes: Everything in moderation.

Next, let's move on and look at the health risks posed by processed or convenience food. Of course, fresh food is far better than processed food.

Packaged food often contains chemicals, such as additives to enhance the colour of the food or preservatives that give the food a longer life. These chemicals aren't good for your health for a number of reasons. First of all, they aren't natural and may perhaps be linked to disease in the long term. And in addition, they may block the body's ability to absorb energy and nutrients from food, with nutrients being the essential vitamins and minerals that are required for healthy bodily function. Finally, let's have a look at nutritional requirements for adults. Here, by "adult," I mean people from 19 to 50 years of age. Let's think about this for a moment. Do you think that energy requirements . . . I mean in terms of the number of calories consumed . . . do you think they are higher for teenagers or adults?

STUDENT: Isn't it true that teenagers would probably need more calories than adults . . . because, I mean, teenagers are still in their growing phase, aren't they?

TEACHER: Yes! It's absolutely true that compared to children and teenagers, energy requirements for adults are lower for both men and women. Nevertheless, the nutritional requirements for vitamins and minerals for adults remain unchanged compared to teenage years. Of course, women experience increased nutritional requirements during pregnancy.

LISTENING PRACTICE TEST 3

SECTION 2 – ANSWERS AND EXPLANATIONS

9) The correct answer is "carbohydrate". The teacher explains that "these four groups are carbohydrate, fruit, vegetables and protein. The first of the four groups [is] *carbohydrate*".

10) The correct answer is "cereals". The teacher says: "The first of the four groups, carbohydrate, includes food like potatoes, bread and *cereals*".

11) The correct answer is "energy". The teacher makes the following comment about carbohydrates: "They provide the building blocks for supplying *energy* to the body".

12) The correct answer is "vegetables". The teacher says: "The second and third food groups are fruit and *vegetables* – although some people would just include these as one group".

13) The correct answer is "variety". The teacher adds that "good nutrition depends on eating a *variety* of fruit and vegetables".

14) The correct answer is 5. The teacher says: "Most medical practitioners in the United States now recommend a minimum consumption of 5 portions of fruit or vegetables every day".

15) The correct answer is "dairy". The teacher comments: "Protein includes food such as meat and fish, as well as *dairy* products, like milk and cheese".

16) The correct answer is "cream". The teacher says: "It's best to limit the consumption of red meat, rich cheeses and *cream*".

17) The correct answer is C. Sugar consumption should be limited. The student correctly comments that "the thing is, to try to be careful not to eat too much sugar".

18) The correct answer is A. The teacher supports his statement about food additives and chemicals by giving reasons for their dangers. He says: "Packaged food often contains chemicals, such as additives to enhance the colour of the food or preservatives that give the food a longer life. These chemicals aren't good for your health for a number of reasons. First of all, they aren't natural and may perhaps be linked to disease in the long term. And in addition, they may block the body's ability to absorb energy and nutrients from food, with nutrients being the essential vitamins and minerals that are required for healthy bodily function".

19) The correct answer is B. The statement that processed and convenience foods may damage the health is true according to the

discussion. The teacher says: "let's move on and look at the health risks posed by processed or convenience food".

LISTENING PRACTICE TEST 3

SECTION 3 – LISTENING TEXT

Teacher: Good afternoon, everyone. In our seminar today, we're going to be discussing educational strategies. Since all of you are studying education and are going to be teachers yourselves one day, I'm sure you can appreciate that this is a very worthwhile topic for discussion. It goes without saying that I hope everyone has read the background reading for today! . . . Of course, as teachers, you will be able to use a very wide variety of assessment models. Let's look at the pedagogical approach that we are going to discuss: the student readiness model.

So what do we mean by the student readiness model? Well, as teachers you'll quickly realise that students are individuals, each operating at different levels of ability. For some students, this might mean that they are operating above the average ability level of their contemporaries, while for others . . . um . . . they may be functioning at a level that is below average. Then, too, there are the students who are in what can be called a "comfort zone" . . . these students are learning at the optimum learning level: they are being challenged and learning new things, but yet they don't feel overwhelmed or inundated by the new information.

Okay . . . just to complicate things, we also have to remember that student readiness is not a static entity. In other words, it is constantly changing. Some students will become more confident throughout the semester and will be able to increase their "student readiness". And, unfortunately, other students may fall behind and might slip to a below-average position. Therefore, the onus falls on us as teachers not only to work out how best to design the curriculum, but also how to structure classroom learning activities that are going to challenge the maximum amount of students. As you will have discovered in your reading for today, the strategy of "question adjustment" can be deployed to help bridge the gap between those students with low readiness and those with high readiness. Now . . . based on the reading, who can explain the concept of "question adjustment"?

Student: If I have understood the reading for today correctly, "question adjustment" means that the teacher will ask questions at a variety of different levels of difficulty. There will be some so-called "easy" questions to build the confidence of the students who are less ready. And then, there will also be some really difficult questions, which are supposed to stretch the more capable students, who are the most ready. . . . Did I get that right?

Teacher: Yes, that's perfect! Now can you expand on that point? I'm thinking here about learning materials that can be used in the classroom in order to achieve "question adjustment" . . .

Student: I think I'm with you . . . Are you alluding to what they . . . uh . . . said in the book about posters? That thing about putting up posters in the . . . uh . . . classroom with some of the questions on them, and making sure that each poster has a question of a different level of difficulty?

Teacher: Yes! I can see that you are really very well prepared for today's discussion. Great! Now, let's move on to the area of formal assessment, in other words, quizzes and tests and so on. Of course, we should distinguish here between "formal" and "informal". Can anyone explain the difference?

Student: The formal ones are those that count towards the mark or grade for the course.

Teacher: Fantastic! So, as I'm sure you know, the purpose of giving the informal assessment is, again, to help build student confidence. Readiness begets confidence, but conversely, confidence can also help to improve a student's level of readiness.

LISTENING PRACTICE TEST 3

SECTION 3 – ANSWERS AND EXPLANATIONS

20) The correct answer is "student readiness model". The teacher says: "So let's look at the pedagogical approach that we are going to discuss today: the *student readiness model*".

21) The correct answer is "levels of ability". The teacher comments that "you'll quickly realise that students are individuals, each operating at different *levels of ability*".

22) The correct answer is "optimum learning level". The teacher says: "There are the students who are in what can be called a 'comfort zone' . . . these students are learning at the *optimum learning level*".

23) The correct answer is B. The teacher supports her statement that student readiness is not a static entity by explaining the ways in which a student's level can change. She says: "We also have to remember that student readiness is not a static entity. In other words, it is constantly changing. Some students will become more confident throughout the semester and will be able to increase their 'student readiness'. And, unfortunately, other students may fall behind and might slip to a below-average position".

24) The correct answer is A. The teacher states that it is the duty of the teachers to decide which curriculum design is best. She comments that "the onus falls on us as teachers not only to work out how best to design the curriculum, but also how to structure classroom learning activities that are going to challenge the maximum amount of students". "Onus" means duty or responsibility.

25) The correct answer is B. The statement that the teacher should ask questions at various levels of difficulty is the best description of the "question adjustment" strategy. The student correctly responds that "question adjustment means that the teacher will ask questions at a variety of different levels of difficulty. There will be some so-called 'easy' questions to build the confidence of the students who are less ready. And then, there will also be some really difficult questions, which are supposed to stretch the more capable students, who are the most ready".

26) The correct answer is A. Posters can be used in the question adjustment strategy. The student correctly remarks about "that thing about putting up posters in the . . . uh . . . classroom with some of the questions on them, and making sure that each poster has a question of a different level of difficulty".

27) The correct answer is A. Formal assessment is given to students because it counts for a mark. The student explains that "the formal ones are those that count towards the mark or grade for the course".

28) The correct answer is C. The purpose of informal assessment is to build student confidence. The teacher explains that "the purpose of giving the informal assessment is, again, to help build student confidence".

29) The correct answer is C. According to the discussion, student confidence enhances student readiness. The teacher concludes the discussion by explaining that "confidence can also help to improve a student's level of readiness".

LISTENING PRACTICE TEST 3

SECTION 4 – LISTENING TEXT

Antarctica is a mysterious and resilient continent that is often forgotten by virtue of its geographical location. The Antarctic is remote and desolate. Nevertheless, an understanding of this continent is critical to our comprehension of the world as a global community. For this reason, the southernmost continent has been the source of a great deal of scientific investigation.

Scientists who have explored this barren land have come from around the world. In 1907, Ernest Shackleton led one of the first expeditions in this area. One of the groups under his supervision was the first to summit Mount Erebus. Shackleton and three other members of his team made several records in the three month period from December 1908 to February 1909. They were the first human beings to travel across the Transantarctic Mountain Range, as well as the first to reach the South Polar Plateau.

In December 1911, Roald Amundsen, a Norwegian explorer, was the first to reach the geographic South Pole, having journeyed via the Bay of Whales and the Axel Heiberg Glacier. Richard Evelyn Byrd also led several explorations of the Antarctic by air throughout the 1930s and 1940s. He then implemented land transport and conducted biological and geographical studies. Later, on October 31, 1956, an expedition led by Rear Admiral George Dufek of the United States Navy successfully landed an aeroplane on the continent. In addition, much notable recent research has come from America and Great Britain.

This corpus of research has resulted in an abundance of factual data on the Antarctic. Containing nearly seventy percent of the world's freshwater supply, Antarctica plays a crucial role in the world's ecosphere. Therefore, the Antarctic is also a key factor in current global climate change. On its surface, it possesses a four kilometre thick ice sheet. This mammoth sheet of ice atrophies because of year-round melting at its base, as well as the loss of ice due to the formation of icebergs. However, the ice sheet is also perpetually replenished by snowfall and frost.

At present, two methodologies are employed to measure the size of the ice sheet. The first is the accumulation method, by which the difference between the loss of ice and the accumulation of new precipitation is calculated. The second technique, known as the direct measurement approach, involves the use of satellites to determine whether the ice sheet is growing thicker. Unfortunately, both methods have a rather large potential for error.

The measurement of the ice sheet is of paramount importance because scientists fear that the melting of a large amount of the ice sheet may occur as a result of global warming. Some believe that human beings are directly responsible for any potential ecological catastrophe, pointing to their excessive reliance on fossil fuels for domestic use and transportation. On the other hand, some assert that natural causes also have a part to play in the debacle, especially volcanic eruptions. While there are some uncertainties about the phenomenon of global warming, it is indisputable that the current rate of sea level change is unprecedented.

LISTENING PRACTICE TEST 3

SECTION 4 – ANSWERS AND EXPLANATIONS

30) The correct answer is "mountains". The speaker comments that "Shackleton and three other members of his team made several records in the three month period from December 1908 to February 1909. They were the first human beings to travel across the Transantarctic *Mountain Range*, as well as the first to reach the South Polar Plateau". Note that you need to change the noun phrase "mountain range" to "mountains" in order to fit within the word limit, as well as to make the phrase grammatically correct.

31) The correct answer is "geographic". The speaker says: "In December 1911, Roald Amundsen, a Norwegian explorer, was the first to reach the *geographic* South Pole".

32) Possible correct answers are: 1940 / 1940s. The speaker explains that "Richard Evelyn Byrd also led several explorations of the Antarctic by air throughout the 1930s and 1940s".

33) The correct answer is "transport". The speaker adds: "He then implemented land *transport* and conducted biological and geographical studies".

34) The correct answer is "aeroplane". The speaker continues as follows: "On October 31, 1956, an expedition led by Rear Admiral George Dufek of the United States Navy successfully landed an *aeroplane* on the continent".

35) The correct answer is C. Melting causes atrophy of the Antarctic ice sheet. The speaker says: "This mammoth sheet of ice atrophies because of year-round melting at its base".

36) The correct answer is B. Both methods used to measure the size of the ice sheet may result in errors. The speaker comments: "Unfortunately, both methods have a rather large potential for error".

37) The correct answer is B. Measurement of the ice sheet is important because of global warming. The speaker says: "The measurement of the ice sheet is of paramount importance because scientists fear that the melting of a large amount of the ice sheet may occur as a result of global warming".

38-40) The correct answers are: B, C and E. The following three statements give the main ideas from the talk: (B) There have been several important expeditions to the Antarctic in the twentieth and twenty-first centuries; (C) The expeditions to the Antarctic have resulted in many important scientific discoveries; and (E) Scientific discoveries about the

Antarctic help us to understand the world's ecosphere. Answers B, C and E are the best because they are the most general. We know from the word "several" in statement B, "many" in statement C and "discoveries" in statement E that generalisations are being given to express main ideas. Statements (A) and (D) are specific points form the lecture, not main ideas.

IELTS Practice Listening – Test 4
Answer Sheet

1.
2.
3.
4.
5.
6.
7.
8.
9.
10.
11.
12.
13.
14.
15.
16.
17.
18.
19.
20.

21.
22.
23.
24.
25.
26.
27.
28.
29.
30.
31.
32.
33.
34.
35.
36.
37.
38.
39.
40

IELTS Practice Listening – Test 4

LISTENING PRACTICE TEST 4

SECTION 1   **QUESTIONS 1 – 10**

Questions 1-4: Complete the sentences in the notes below, using **ONLY ONE WORD OR NUMBER** in each gap.

---

1) Lewis and Clark were two famous _____ of the American West.

2) What year did the two men began their expedition westward? _____

3) The area of the United States was then known as the Louisiana _____.

4) What year was Lewis was born? _____

Questions 5-10: Choose the correct letter A, B or C.

5)   How did Lewis and Clark become friends?

   A. They were neighbours.

   B. They worked in the same branch of the government

   C. They were in the same local division of the army.

6) Who offered Lewis the job of exploring the west?

   A. Jefferson

   B. Clark

   C. Congress

7) Why did Clark travel with Lewis?

   A. Lewis felt he needed a partner.

   B. Clark felt he needed a partner.

   C. Because of financial restrictions.

8) Why were Lewis and Clark good as partners?

   A. They each had different personal characteristics.

   B. They were dissimilar in temperament.

   C. They shared many traits and abilities.

9) How long did the journey last?

   A. Eight thousand miles

   B. Three and a half years

   C. Eighty thousand miles

10) What happened after the expedition had finished?

    A. Clark died unexpectedly.

    B. The Louisiana Territory was purchased.

    C. The Missouri River was discovered.

SECTION 2　　QUESTIONS 11 – 20

Questions 11-12: Choose 2 letters from A – E below that the speaker mentions about cancer in the first part of the listening passage.

11-12) Which of the following statements are true according to the passage? For this question, **CHOOSE TWO ANSWERS**.

　　A. Cancer is a group of more than 100 different diseases.

　　B. Cells in the body normally divide without control or order.

　　C. The body produces more cells when needed.

　　D. Internal organs help prevent the spread of cancer.

　　E. Tumours usually cannot be removed.

Questions 13-20: Choose the correct letter A, B or C.

13)　How are tumours formed?

　　A. from the abnormal growth of organs

　　B. when cells divide

　　C. when cells form without order

14)　What is metastasis?

　　A. the spread of cancer from a tumour

　　B. the growth of cancer in a cell

　　C. the growth of cancer inside a tumour

15) What is the biggest cause of cancer?

   A. poor nutrition

   B. overexposure to the sun

   C. smoking

16) What advice did the speaker NOT provide about avoiding skin cancer?

   A. To use sun cream

   B. To wear a hat

   C. To avoid the sun in the middle of the day

17) How does cancer compare to other diseases?

   A. It is the first leading cause of death.

   B. It is the second leading cause of death.

   C. It is the third leading cause of death.

18) How many women will eventually develop cancer?

   A. one-fourth

   B. one-third

   C. 13%

19) How many men develop cancer during their lifetimes?

   A. one-fourth

   B. one-half

   C. 5%

20) What is the main purpose of this lecture?

   A. To show that people themselves are usually to blame for getting cancer.

   B. To provide information and facts about cancer

   C. To criticise those who fail to get treatment for their cancer.

SECTION 3   QUESTIONS 21 – 30

Questions 21-24

Complete the chart below. Write **ONLY ONE WORD OR NUMBER** in each gap.

The Four Key Problems Areas of Philosophy:	
First problem area:	human **21)** _____
Second problem area:	human **22)** _____
Third problem area:	human **23)** _____
Fourth problem area:	the **24)** _____ of the human being

Questions 25-27: Choose the correct letter A, B or C.

25) Which question is central to this philosophical investigation?

   A. Can human beings make choices that will alter their futures?

   B. Are human beings capable of making good decisions?

   C. Why do human beings have to choose?

26) What is epistemology?

   A. the study of being

   B. the study of knowledge

   C. the study of decision making

27) What aspects of human personality are NOT investigated?

    A. emotional

    B. spiritual

    C. physiological

Questions 28-30: Complete each sentence, using **NO MORE THAN THREE WORDS**.

28) The study of the philosophy of human nature should enable an individual to contemplate more deeply . . . .

29) The study of philosophy includes and engagement with these three kinds of debates: . . . .

30) Not surprisingly, the works of Plato and Aristotle are generally regarded as the . . . . for this subject.

SECTION 4   QUESTIONS 31 – 40

Questions 31-33

Complete the chart below. Write **ONLY ONE WORD OR NUMBER** in each gap.

The Olympic Games - Notes	
When did the first official Olympic Games take place?	31) _____
How many events did the Pentathlon include?	32) _____
Who was not allowed to compete in the ancient Olympic Games?	33) _____

Questions 34-40: Choose the correct letters A, B, C, or D.

34) What is the IOC?

   A. International Olympic Committee

   B. International Official City

   C. International Olympic City

35-36) For this question, **CHOOSE TWO ANSWERS**.

   What are the purposes of the IOC?

   A. to establish the program of events

   B. to ensure that all countries are fairly represented

   C. to choose the city where the games take place

   D. to monitor the participation of athletes

37-38) *For this question,* **CHOOSE TWO ANSWERS**.

What happens during "The Parade of Nations"?

A. athletes begin to compete

B. athletes march around the stadium

C. athletes take the Olympic Oath

D. athletes represent their countries

39) What is the purpose of the Olympic Games?

A. To oversee athletes from various countries

B. To make money on a national level

C. To promote friendship among the nations

40) What is the main point of this discussion?

A. to discuss the history and background of the Olympics

B. to describe the relationship of Greek Emperors to the Olympics

C. to explain why the ancient Olympic games were banned

ANSWER KEY – LISTENING PRACTICE TEST 4

1) explorers

2) 1804

3) Territory

4) 1774

5) C

6) A

7) A

8) C

9) A

10) B

11-12) A and C

13) C

14) A

15) C

16) B

17) B

18) B

19) B

20) B

21) choice

22) thought

23) personality

24) unity

25) A

26) B

27) C

28) vital human issues

29) political, cultural, social

30) foundation

31) 1896

32) 5

33) women

34) A

35-36) A and C

37-38) B and D

39) C

40) A

TEXTS, ANSWERS AND EXPLANATIONS

LISTENING PRACTICE TEST 4

SECTION 1 – LISTENING TEXT

Meriwether Lewis and William Clark were perhaps the two most famous explorers of the American West. In 1804, the two men began an expedition westward across the area of the United States that was then known as the Louisiana Territory, and along their way, they encountered unknown people and harsh climatic conditions.

Lewis was born on August 18, 1774, in the state of Virginia. Clark was also born in Virginia, although he was four years older than Lewis. The two men met when Lewis joined the local militia, of which Clark was in command. During their experiences in combat, Lewis and Clark made a long-lasting friendship.

Unites States President Thomas Jefferson had been Lewis's neighbour, and when Lewis was a young captain in the army, he received a letter from Jefferson offering him a job in charge of an expedition to explore the Western country.

On February 28, 1803, the United States Congress finally approved the financing for the expedition. At this time, Lewis told President Jefferson that it would be preferable to have a partner for the rigorous journey westward. With Jefferson's permission, Lewis offered the assignment to his friend Clark.

In terms of their backgrounds, abilities, and interests, Lewis and Clark had a great deal in common. They both possessed many traits that would prove to be crucial for such a daunting expedition: they were intelligent, courageous, and loved adventure, and because of their time in the army, they were calm under pressure and able to make important decisions quickly.

The journey that Lewis and Clark made was more than 8,000 miles in length and lasted for nearly two and a half years. The team charted their course by following the Missouri River, and they were responsible for discovering the Northwest Passage. When their expedition had safely concluded, President Jefferson purchased the Louisiana Territory for fifteen million dollars.

Tragically, Lewis died at the age of 35, only three years after the expedition had finished. Clark lived a long and prosperous life in the state of Missouri, where he died peacefully in 1838. It is commonly believed that both men are worthy of laud and praise, providing later generations with an example of heroic patriotism and nationalistic vision.

LISTENING PRACTICE TEST 4

SECTION 1 – ANSWERS AND EXPLANATIONS

1) The correct answer is: explorers. The passage begins as follows: "Meriwether Lewis and William Clark were perhaps the two most famous explorers of the American West."

2) The correct answer is: 1804. In the introduction to the lecture, the speaker states: "In 1804, the two men began an expedition westward . . . "

3) The correct answer is: Territory. The speaker explains that the journey was across "the area of the United States that was then known as the Louisiana Territory."

4) The correct answer is: 1774. In the second paragraph of the text of the lecture, the speaker says that "Lewis was born on August 18, 1774, in the state of Virginia."

5) The correct answer is C. Lewis and Clark became friends because they were in the same local division of the army. The speaker states: "The two men met when Lewis joined the local militia."

6) The correct answer is A. Jefferson offered Lewis the job of exploring the west. The speaker explains that "when Lewis was a young captain in the

army, he received a letter from Jefferson offering him a job in charge of an expedition to explore the Western country."

7) The correct answer is A. Clark travelled with Lewis because Lewis felt he needed a partner. The lecturer comments that "Lewis told President Jefferson that it would be preferable to have a partner for the rigorous journey westward. With Jefferson's permission, Lewis offered the assignment to his friend Clark. "

8) The correct answer is C. Lewis and Clark were good as partners because they shared many traits and abilities. The speaker states: "They both possessed many traits that would prove to be crucial for such a daunting expedition."

9) The correct answer is A. The speaker explains that "the journey that Lewis and Clark made was more than 8,000 miles in length and lasted for nearly two and a half years."

10) The correct answer is B. The Louisiana Territory was purchased after the expedition had finished. The speaker says that "when their expedition had safely concluded, President Jefferson purchased the Louisiana Territory."

LISTENING PRACTICE TEST 4

SECTION 2 – LISTENING TEXT

Cancer, a group of more than 100 different types of disease, occurs when cells in the body begin to divide abnormally and continue dividing and forming more cells without control or order. Importantly, all internal organs of the body consist of cells, which normally divide to produce more cells when the body requires them. This is a natural, orderly process that keeps human beings healthy.

However, if a cell divides when it is not necessary, a large growth called a tumour can form. These tumours can usually be removed, and in many cases, they do not come back. Unfortunately, in some cases the cancer from the original tumour spreads. The spread of cancer in this way is called metastasis.

There are some factors which are known to increase the risk of cancer. Smoking is the largest single cause of death from cancer. One-third of the deaths from cancer each year are related to smoking, making tobacco use the most preventable cause of death.

Choice of food can also be linked to cancer. Research shows that there is a link between high-fat food and certain cancers, and being seriously overweight is also a cancer risk. Cancer risk can therefore be reduced by cutting down on fatty food and eating generous amounts of fruit and vegetables.

Skin cancer is the most common type of cancer for both men and women. Repeated exposure to the sun, through sunbathing for example, greatly increases a person's chance of developing this kind of cancer. As a general rule, it is usually best to avoid the sun during the midday and early afternoon, but when this is not possible, one should be sure to use protective sun-blocking creams.

Cancer is now the second leading cause of death. One-third of all women and half of all men will develop some form of cancer during their lifetimes. Yet, millions of people have been successfully treated for cancer. The sooner cancer is found and treatment starts, the better one's chances are for successfully treating the cancer and living a long and healthy life.

LISTENING PRACTICE TEST 4

SECTION 2 – ANSWERS AND EXPLANATIONS

11-12) The correct answers are A and C. In the first part of the talk, the speaker explains that "Cancer [is] a group of more than 100 different types of disease" and that cells "normally divide to produce more cells when the body requires them."

13) The correct answer is C. When discussing tumours, the speaker states that "if a cell divides when it is not necessary, a large growth called a tumour can form."

14) The correct answer is A. Metastasis is the spread of cancer from a tumour. The lecturer explains that "in some cases the cancer from the original tumour spreads. The spread of cancer in this way is called metastasis."

15) The correct answer is C. Smoking is the biggest cause of cancer. The speaker comments that "smoking is the largest single cause of death from cancer."

16) The correct answer is B. The speaker gives this advice: "As a general rule, it is usually best to avoid the sun during midday and early afternoon, but when this is not possible, one should be sure to use protective sun-blocking creams." Wearing a hat is not mentioned.

17) The correct answer is B. Cancer is the second leading cause of death. In the final paragraph of the lecture text, the speaker states that "cancer is now the second leading cause of death."

18) The correct answer is B. One-third of women will eventually develop cancer. The speaker says: "One-third of all women and half of all men will develop some form of cancer during their lifetimes."

19) The correct answer is B. One-half of men will develop cancer. The speaker says: "One-third of all women and half of all men will develop some form of cancer during their lifetimes."

20) The correct answer is B. The lecture is full of facts, statistics, and examples. So, the main purpose of the talk is to provide information and facts.

LISTENING PRACTICE TEST 4

SECTION 3 – LISTENING TEXT

The study of the philosophy of human nature is often regarded as an investigation into the meaning of life. This subject usually deals with four key problem areas: human choice, human thought, human personality, and the unity of the human being. A consideration of these four problem areas can also include scientific and artistic viewpoints on the nature of human life.

The first problem area, human choice, asks whether human beings can really make decisions that can change their futures. Conversely, it investigates to what extent the individual's future is fixed and pre-determined by cosmic forces outside the control of human beings.

In the second problem area, human thought, epistemology is considered. Epistemology means the study of knowledge; it should not be confused with ontology, the study of being or existence.

The third key issue, human personality, emphasizes aspects of human life that are beyond mental processes. It takes a look at emotional, spiritual, and communal elements. Importantly, the study of the communal aspect focuses on community and communication, rather than on government or the philosophy of the state.

Finally, the fourth problem, the unity of the human being, explores the first three areas more fully and asks whether there is any unifying basis for human choice, thought, and personality. In other words, while the human is an inherently complex being, there must be a unity or wholeness underlying these complications.

The study of the philosophy of human nature should enable an individual to contemplate more deeply vital human issues, including an engagement with political, cultural, and social debates. Not surprisingly, the works of Plato and Aristotle are generally regarded as the foundation for this subject.

LISTENING PRACTICE TEST 4

SECTION 3 – ANSWERS AND EXPLANATIONS

21) The correct answer is: choice. At the beginning of the lecture, the speaker states: "This subject usually deals with four key problem areas: human choice, human thought, human personality, and the unity of the human being." These subject areas are repeated at the start of each paragraph in the lecture text.

22) The correct answer is: thought. The speaker comments: "In the second problem area, human thought, epistemology is considered."

23) The correct answer is: personality. The speaker says: "The third key issue, human personality, emphasizes aspects of human life that are beyond mental processes."

24) The correct answer is: unity. Later in the lecture, the speaker states: "Finally, the fourth problem, the unity of the human being, explores the first three areas more fully . . ."

25) The correct answer is A. The following question is central to the investigation of human choice: "Can human beings make choices that will alter their futures? The speaker states: "The first problem area, human

choice, asks whether human beings can really make decisions that can change their futures."

26) The correct answer is B. Epistemology is the study of knowledge. In paragraph three of the lecture text, the speaker explains that "epistemology means the study of knowledge."

27) The correct answer is C. The emotional and spiritual aspects of human personality are investigated. The speaker states: "The third key issue, human personality, emphasizes aspects of human life that are beyond mental processes. It takes a look at emotional, spiritual, and communal elements." Physiological aspects are not mentioned.

28) The correct answer is: vital human issues. In the last paragraph of the lecture text, the speaker states: "The study of the philosophy of human nature should enable an individual to contemplate more deeply vital human issues."

29) The correct answer is: political, cultural, social. In the final paragraph, the speaker says that the study of philosophy also includes "an engagement with political, cultural, and social debates"

30) The correct answer is: foundation. The speaker concludes the talk as follows: "Not surprisingly, the works of Plato and Aristotle are generally regarded as the foundation for this subject."

LISTENING PRACTICE TEST 4

SECTION 4 – LISTENING TEXT

The Olympic Games have a long and rich history. The first official Olympic Games took place in Athens in 1896, although experts point out that there is evidence of ancient Olympic Games taking place as early as 776 BC. Athletes in these ancient games competed on the plains of the Greek city of Olympia. The ancient Olympic Games were part of a religious festival and continued for nearly twelve centuries, until banned by Byzantine Emperor Theodosius in 393 AD.

The ancient Olympic Games consisted of several athletic events. Perhaps the most gruelling sport was the Pentathlon, an event which included five parts: running, jumping, wrestling, boxing, and the discus throw. The ancient games also included equestrian events, such as horse and chariot racing.

While women were forbidden to compete or even to enter the stadium during the ancient games, many female athletes compete in various events in today's Olympic Games. In addition, although only Greek-born men were allowed to compete in the ancient games, men and women from all over the world come to compete and represent their countries in the modern Olympic Games.

Nowadays, the Olympic Games are governed and organized on an international level by the International Olympic Committee, known as the IOC. The IOC establishes the program of events and chooses the city in which the games are to be held. On the national level, each country that sends athletes to the games has a National Olympic Committee that oversees the participation of the athletes for their countries.

The opening ceremony of the games is held in a stadium in a major city. After the parade of nations, in which the athletes march around the stadium to represent their host country, the athletes take the Olympic Oath. The games, which are said to promote friendship and understanding among nations, then officially begin.

LISTENING PRACTICE TEST 4

SECTION 4 – ANSWERS AND EXPLANATIONS

31) The correct answer is: 1896. The speaker states: "The first official Olympic Games took place in Athens in 1896."

32) The correct answer is: 5. The Pentathlon included five events. The speaker explains that "perhaps the most grueling sport was the Pentathlon, an event which included five parts."

33) The correct answer is: women. Women were not allowed to compete in the ancient Olympic Games. The speaker comments that "women were forbidden to compete or even to enter the stadium during the ancient games." The phrase "non-Greek men" would be incorrect because you are allowed only one word in the gap.

34) The correct answer is A. The IOC is the International Olympic Committee. The speaker states that "the Olympic Games are governed and organized on an international level by the International Olympic Committee, known as the IOC."

35-36) The correct answers are A and C. The speaker states: "The IOC establishes the program of events and chooses the city in which the games are to be held."

37-38) The correct answers are B and D. The speaker says that during "the parade of nations, [. . .] the athletes march around the stadium to represent their host country."

39) The correct answer is C. The purpose of the Olympic Games is to promote friendship among the nations. The speaker states: "The games [. . .] are said to promote friendship and understanding among nations."

40) The correct answer is A. The main point of the lecture is to discuss the history and background of the Olympics. In the first sentence of the lecture, the speaker introduces the topic as follows: "The Olympic Games have a long and rich history."